FORGIVE US OUR KING

Healing for Your Soul

Cheryl Elaine Dowdell

ISBN 978-1-968970-05-5 (Paperback)
ISBN 978-1-968970-06-2 (Ebook)

Inquiries and Book Orders should be addressed to:

Leavitt Peak Press
17901 Pioneer Blvd Ste L #298, Artesia, California 90701
Phone #: 2092191548

An Inspirational Speaker

Giving honor to Jesus Christ who rules and super rule in my life. I received Jesus Christ in my life at the age of eight years old at Mount Calvary Baptist Church on Spruce Street in Jacksonville, Florida. Looking back over my life, it would be very easy to assume that I lived a painful life. I must disagree because Jesus Christ has been with me all the days of my life. In my King James Study Bible, the book of Matthew 28:20 tells us to observe all things whatever Jesus have commanded us, and he would be with us alway (meaning there is only one way) even unto the end of the world. Life has taught me to follow Christ and Christ alone.

Everything and everyone has meaning when you connect it to Christ. No matter if a situation is good or bad, it has meaning. After Christ ascended to be at the right hand of his Father, He said the Holy Ghost would come, and we would be witnesses in his name all over this earth. Nothing catches Jesus Christ by surprise, Isaiah 46:10 says his Father knows the end of a situation from the beginning. Even in the worst situation anyone can imagine, it can turn out to be a blessing. John 15:5 tells us without Jesus, we can do nothing, meaning before evil was plotted against you, the enemy had to get his permission from Jesus Christ.

Romans 8:28 tells us that all things work together for good to them that love God and to them who are the called according to his purpose. So, this means whatever we face in life we can get over it if we put our trust in Jesus Christ. John 3:16 says, "For God so loved the world, that He gave His only begotten Son, that whosoever believeth in Him should not perish, but have everlasting life." This is why we can all be saved. Romans 10:9 says, "If you confess with your mouth that Jesus is Lord and believe in your heart that God raised

Jesus from the dead, you can be saved today, this is how we become saved."

As you read what the Lord has laid on my heart to share with you, you will understand why I took the time to write this information on paper. I feel in my heart that God created me to worship Him and not man. For it is written in John 16:33 that Jesus says, "These things I have spoken unto you that in Me you might have peace. In the world you shall have trouble; but be of good cheer, I have overcome the world." It is not possible to live life without ever having trouble, but it is possible to conquer every obstacle that you will ever face in life. To make this a reality in your life is to accept Jesus Christ as Lord and Savior of your life today. Your name must be written in the Lambs Book of Life, so please read Revelation 20:11–15. All of the prophecies have already been fulfilled except one, and that one is the coming of Jesus Christ to take us to our eternal home by way of rapture.

The rapture is a term used by certain Christians, referring to an end-time when all Christian believers who are living and dead will rise into the sky and join Christ. This information can be found in 1 Thessalonians 13:13–18, it says:

> But I would not have you to be ignorant, brethren, concerning them which are asleep, that you sorrow not, even as others which have no hope. For if we believe that Jesus died and rose again, even those which sleep in Jesus will God bring with Him. For this we say unto you by the word of the Lord, that we which are alive and remain unto the coming of the Lord shall not prevent them which are asleep. For the Lord Himself shall descend from heaven with a shout, with the voice of the archangel and with the trump of God: and the dead in Christ shall rise first: Then we which are alive and remain shall be caught up in the clouds, to meet the Lord in the air: and so shall we ever be with the Lord. Wherefore comfort one another with these words.

SURRENDERING TO THE WILL OF GOD

Sunday July 16, 2017, at 9:30 p.m., I said to the Holy Spirit, "Have your way in my life, it is alright for you to take complete control." After accepting the fact that marrying my third husband wasn't the answer and my daughter's relationship with me was based on a lie from the pits of hell, I surrendered unto the Lord to write this book. In July 2012, the Holy Ghost was speaking to me daily, concerning the conditions of this world. He said to me that "I must feed His sheep." I heard him loud and clear. I set up a meeting with my Senior Pastor at that time to let him know that the Lord had spoken to me again. The first time I heard the voice of the Lord was in 2004. I told my Pastor that the Lord was calling me to go out in the community to call His people in. The Pastor's response to me was, "Who is going to listen?" I went away, feeling like maybe that voice was not the voice of the Lord. Deep down in my soul, I knew that it was the voice of the Lord.

From 2004–2017, the Holy Spirit would speak to me often no matter where I was or what I may have been doing at the time. For example, if I was doing the dishes, the Holy Spirit would visit me. If I was asleep, the Holy Spirit would wake me up 2:00 a.m. or 3:00 a.m. It did not matter what time it was. He would engage in conversations about the world and its condition. Most of all, he was concerned about his people. I remember saying to the Holy Spirit, "They will not listen to you but, I will listen to you." I also remember saying to the Holy Spirit, "I will be your legs to walk and I will be your mouth to talk." Soon after the conversation, the Holy Spirit went away.

The following Sunday, I was at church, the Bishop preached a sermon called, "The Anatomy of an Announcement," taken from Mark 11:1–19. At the end of the sermon, I remember the congregation were in high worship mode. The Holy Spirit came and said in my ear, "You said you would be my legs to walk."

I said quietly, "Oh, my Lord, is that you?"

The Holy Spirit said "you said you would be my mouth to talk."

I said quietly, "Please, Holy Spirit, if this is not you, please don't make me go."

Then the Holy Spirit said, "Go!"

I got up from my seat and went toward the podium where the Bishop was standing. He was up higher than where I was standing. He did not see me coming. I remember reaching up my hand toward him. The Bishop stepped back, drew back the microphone, and said "I can't give this to you." I was in the Spirit but not out of my mind. I went back to my seat. The Bishop interpreted that I was asking for the microphone. I believe the Lord was asking for the microphone.

Again, I went away thinking maybe it wasn't God, but deep down, I knew that it was Him. Around this same time, the Lord was showing me different things that has come to past. I labored on my job for twenty plus years at Shands Jacksonville in Jacksonville, Florida. I loved my Job, coworkers, patients, families, and etc. It is just my nature to love people. When you enter into the main entrance of Shands Hospital, on the wall to your left says, "My Shands Jacksonville." You'll see my name engraved in it, "Cheryl Flowers." It was a campaign that Tracee came up with to raise money for the hospital. I said that to say this. I was so dedicated to my job until I thought it not robbery to help in a situation when I really could not afford it, but I did any way. That is how much I loved my job. Because the Lord had a work for me to do in the community, he orchestrated a situation that was not even in my character to have me terminated to do his will. The Lord knew I loved my job and his people too much to quit or leave Shands.

I truly believed that the Lord had work for me to do concerning His people. Everyone who knew me at Shands knew my conversation was about Jesus Christ and Him being crucified for us because

He loved us so much. I completed the job I was sent to do at Shands Jacksonville. The reason I knew it was the Lord orchestrating the situation is because what I was accused of; everyone knew it was not in my character to do such a thing. Days before I was terminated from Shands, I told my husband that I would be getting terminated because the Lord showed it to me in the Spirit. See if this makes since to you. The first seventeen years I labored at Shands, I never was in trouble about nothing. No write-ups, no warnings, and no kind of trouble at all the first seventeen years.

I transferred to the Transitional Care Unit, the first day in that unit I was placed with the person that was to train me to the unit. The Lord told me that the person who was training me was going to be the one that would get me terminated. On day one, this woman was so mean to me it was a shame. I asked the manager the next morning if there was someone else who could train me; of course there were none. It took her six years to plot against me. After she trained me for about six weeks on a job, I already knew just in a different department. The next day, I gave her a thank you card with a twenty-five-dollar gift card from Walmart. The reason I wanted to bless her is because I wanted to show her love when it was obvious she was being unkind to me. The same person I blessed that did the My Shands Jacksonville campaign that have my name engraved in the wall is the same person that ended my job without further investigation.

Although I knew the Lord wanted to use me as his messenger, I told the Lord just let me finish nursing school and then I would follow his command, but that was a big mistake. The Lord allowed me to finish nursing school. From the time I finished nursing school until now (2018), I had not done what I knew the Lord called me to do. Not living up to my vow I made unto the Lord, he would allow me to get good jobs with benefits but would allow crazy things to happen that would close the doors.

The last job I was terminated from before I decided to finish this book, I was called in the office for one thing that was not a big deal. The Lord intervened again and allowed me to tell on myself and got my own self fired by my director who attends the same church that I attend. When I took this job, I felt like this job was heaven-sent. I ministered to everyone who came cross my path in such a way the anointing was felt by all who heard. I still feel this job is heaven-sent, and while I am trying to get it back, I know that I must do what the Lord is telling me to do.

The situations I have encountered with my jobs and the situations with the Holy Spirit should not be taken likely. Everyone needs a job, and Christ died so we can have eternal life with him. If I worked at Shands for twenty plus years, lifting up the name of Jesus each and every day and on this last job because of the reality of the circumstances, I believe that the Holy Spirit wants to do what He was sent to do if we let Him. This last job I worked for a company called Ascension, I was so grateful to my King for giving me the job to do.

I was in need of a job once again. I sat to the computer to put in applications for employment. Out of all the applications I put in, Ascension called me in for an interview, and they hired me. The name, Ascension, is dear to my heart; they are known as a ministry not a job. They start their morning by opening up with a prayer in Jesus's name. The name of the department I was hired to work in is called the Good Shepherd. I believed I was in the right place, and I was. In life, out of all the people in this world, there are only two kinds of people. They are people of God and people of satan. This chapter leads me to my next chapter. This I think is vital information that could save lives and make many people whole again. I believe this is why God allows us to go through situations in our lifetime.

CREATED TO WORSHIP OUR KING

I was born November 24, 1962, to Willie Johnson and Ruth Lee Spencer in Jacksonville, Florida. My father retired from University Hospital in Jacksonville, Florida. My mother was a cook at Van's Restaurant on Edison Ave in Jacksonville, Florida. On Easter Sunday in 1972, my mother dressed me and my older sisters in all white and sent us to church around the corner at Mt. Calvary Baptist Church on Spruce Street in Jacksonville, Florida. I enjoyed church; it was very interesting to me to hear about Jesus Christ and Him being crucified for us. Although I can't recall one time going to church with my mother or father, I developed a love relationship with the Lord. At the time, I did not know the love was there. After church was over on Easter Sunday in 1972, me and my sisters walked home from church. We were told our mother was taken to the hospital. A few days later, she passed away in the hospital. So the last time I seen her alive was when she got me dressed for church, Easter Sunday morning, in 1972.

Friends and family members came to my aunt's house to bring food and drinks because of my mother's death. My friend, Sylvia Williams, and I were sitting on the sidewalk at the age of ten. She asked me what happened to my mother, I replied, "Oh the Lord was ready for her, and she had to go home to be with him." Never once did I waste time wondering why. I believe because I knew it was the Lord, and it set well with my soul.

Soon after my mother's funeral, my father walked away from me and never looked back. That was when the spirit of abandonment tried to conquer my life, but Jesus Christ had a different plan for me. I was left to live with my grandmother, who was my maternal grandmother (my mother's mother), and other family members. In my opinion, my grandmother was very mean to me. I did not see Christ anywhere in her relationship to me. I knew that one day Christ would allow me to ask her why was she so mean to me.

Keep in mind there are only two kinds of people in this world, people of Jesus Christ and people of satan. Satan never meant for this book to be written because he knew many souls would be saved because of it. Satan has been trying to kill me since I was a child. Around the age of five, I recall my older sister asking my grandmother if she could take me to the store, Aboud's grocery store, that was on the corner of Park and Jackson Street in Brooklyn here in Jacksonville, Florida. She stopped on the way to one of our neighbor's house, his name was EC. He has passed away now, and he was very old. I recall at the time my sister and I went inside of EC'S house. As he was lying her on the floor, he laid me on the couch, and I recall him performing oral sex on me.

I did not know at the time what was happening to me, but over the years everything unfolded. Also, during this same time in my life, I recall many times this same sister when no one was looking she would take me in the room and take a pillow and nearly smother me to death. It was only by the grace of God she did not kill me. That is how I know if God will be for you, that is more than the whole world against you. When she would let me up, one time, I ran out of the room out the front door, and I heard someone bouncing a basketball on the basketball court nearby. I went to see who it was, it was my childhood friend named Jerry Dowdell. I would stand at the fence and watch him enjoy playing basketball by himself. Around thirty-eight years later, he became my husband.

I am not sure after reading this book if he would still be my husband, but at all cost, I must do the will of my Father because Christ alone is worthy. I trust and believe God with my entire life. I do not want it to be a situation when I stand before Christ, and learn at that time He created me to worship Him. And I did not allow Him to have His way.

It wouldn't be right for me to tell what one person did in my childhood and not the others. I believe I was created to help set the captives free. I have forgiven everyone for any and everything that was done to me. The Lord said that I must forgive if I want to be forgiven for my sins I will and have committed. In that same room where Paula nearly smothered me to death, my sister, Rosilyn, had an older male in that same room there to have his way with me. My oldest sister, Linda, when I would go to spend the nights with her and her two children, Linda's husband used to wait until she was asleep and come into our bedroom to touch us inappropriately. When we would go to my aunt's house, her husband, James, used to do the same thing.

I must tell my story, I would like to help as many people as I can with my story. I must help set the captives free. This is what true love is all about. The Spirit of the Lord is upon me. I am going to just let the Lord have his way.

By now, I'm sure you have probably said that this is a very unusual life for anyone to have lived. Jeremiah 29:11 says, "For I know the thoughts that I think towards you, saith the Lord, thoughts of peace, and not of evil, to give you an expected end." Also, Ecclesiastes 3:1 that to everything there is a season and a time to every purpose under the heaven. It would be a blessing to read the entire chapter 3 of Ecclesiastes. I love John 16:33, "It says these things I have spoken unto you, that in me you might have peace. In this world you shall have trouble: be of good cheer; I have over come the world." That is the Lord talking to all of us. This scripture has taught me that no matter what has happened or will happen to me in life, that Jesus Christ has already taken care of it on the cross. We must understand what took place before Jesus went to the cross, while he was on the cross, and what happened when he rose from his grave.

When God raised Jesus from the dead, He rose with all power in His hands. If Christ has all power, this means the only power satan has is the power Christ gives him or the power that we give him. Mark 16:6–7 says, when they went to the grave looking for Jesus's body, the angel said, "Be not afraid: He is risen; He is not here: behold the place where they laid Him. But go your way, tell

His disciples and Peter that He went before you into Galilee; there shall you see Him, as He said unto you." Even though this really did happen, My Lord said in John 10:18 that "no man taketh His life, He has the power to lay it down and pick it up again." He did it for His friends, y'all! Can't you see? This means anyone who believes what is written in his word, especially John 3:16 and Romans 10:9, you shall be saved. Christ also said if He wanted to, He could have called a legion of angels to take Him down off that cross. Instead He allowed them to kill Him so that we might trust in him. Can you explain how could someone that had the kind of life I had could love Christ like I do? The only way this could ever happen is that Christ was there all of the time.

This is the kind of love I have for Christ, not to say I have reached perfection. When it came to His people, when He told me to give, I gave; when He told me to go, I went; and when He told me to say, I said. Even if it was money, house, time-share, husband, job, or daughters, whatever Christ asked of me, I trusted Him with it. Knowing that God is not a man that He should lie, neither is He, the Son of man, that He shall repent. If He spoke it, it will come to pass. What is it you are holding on to and need to let it go?

EXPOSING THE ENEMY

Remember from the previous chapter I shared with you, I was born to Willie Johnson and Ruth Lee Spencer on November 24, 1962. I am the last born of nine children. There were seven different fathers of the nine children. Me and my brother, Sam, the last two of us, had the same father. It wasn't until later in my life I found out about this when I started to question different family members.

The sexual sins were not talked about or dealt with in the family. So to me, that left unexposed demons, running rapid in the atmosphere. Coming up in my days the families kept secrets for whatever their reasons may have been. During this time in my life when things got tough, I was in my car turning into the garage and I begin to cry unto the Lord. I said to the Lord "Lord you know everything, why in the world would you create me, and you knew my life would be as such?" The Lord said immediately, "I created you for me, I am going to use you to help set the captives free." With the Lord's immediate response, my soul has been at peace every since that day.

When I found out that there were seven different fathers, in my mind, I was thinking four different fathers, which was still bad. During the time, I was allowing the Lord to heal me. I attempted to go to where I remembered they buried my mother, but I could not find her grave. At the next gathering our family had, I asked my sisters to come go with me to find our mother's grave. This time was more than thirty years later. We found her grave, and I said a quiet prayer and asked the Lord to forgive my mother for the sins she committed if she had not done so before she died.

I also asked the Lord to help me mend the broken pieces so that all families can be healed if they choose to be healed. After that time,

I began to seek the Lord even more than before and to listen to his lead in my life. I am so glad that I listened to his voice. As you read my story, I know you are saying that I have encountered a lot in life and can write about it to help people heal. Please understand that nothing has, can, or will happen to us in life that God does not know about first. He knows everything. In Revelation 22:13, he tells us he is Alpha and the Omega, the first and the last, the beginning and the end. He knows your name too!

During the time of my life where I found myself hurt, lost, and confused about life and everything in it, my Lord was the only one that was there for me. Remember I did not have a mother, father, grandmother, grandfather, or anyone else I felt I could have gone to. If people haven't been where you have been, or going where you are trying to go, they cannot relate to your circumstances no matter how they try to help. The Lord is the only one that can fix certain situations in your life. Today, I can truly thank God for all my misfortunes I've had in my life because it has made me the woman I am today. I am a strong black woman that is saved, sanctified, and filled with the Holy Spirit because of Jesus Christ. I also have a mind to be ready to be with the Lord when he comes for me.

In my walk with the Lord, I believe that the Bible was written by people who was inspired by the Holy Spirit. The Bible says that we are not to add to or take away from the Bible. I also believe when the enemy convinced Adam and Eve to disobey God in the Garden of Eden, God told Adam that he could eat of every tree in the garden except the tree of the knowledge of good and evil. God told Adam if he eats from the tree the same day, he would surely die.

In my healing process, knowing the reality of my life, my Heavenly Father told me that he chose me to go through everything I had to go through. To prove to the people that even though we do not live in a perfect world and there will be trouble, our Father still expects for us to love one another until he comes for us. He said in his word that eyes have not seen and ears have not heard what he has in store for us.

As it is written in Acts 1:9–11, when Jesus ascended up bodily and visibly, and a cloud received him out of their sight, there were two men standing there and asked the followers of Christ, "Why are they still standing there looking up to Heaven?" The two men told the followers of Christ, just as Christ ascended up the same way, He will return to receive all the other believers unto himself. Just think for a moment, if the followers of Christ could not believe their eyes and the angels had to be present, the only way people would or could believe this story is by faith.

So, in order to expose the enemy, you must agree that there are only two kinds of people that exist in this world in which we live, and they are *believers* and *unbelievers*. For all of the believers they have made up their mind to serve Jesus Christ while they yet live and even after death. For all of the unbelievers they had to come up with a plan to cause as many people as they can to doubt our Lord and Savior, Jesus Christ.

Colossians 4:1–6 teaches us to walk in wisdom. If the unbeliever refuses to believe that which is true by faith means he or she is not wise. The unbeliever cannot be wise because the Bible says in the book of Genesis 1:1, in the "beginning," God created the Heaven and the Earth. Verse 2 says this earth was without form, which means nothing was here before God got here, which means God has always been. Genesis 1:26 says, "Let *us* make man in our image." I will not take it for granted that everyone who is reading this book will know the *us* who God is speaking of. The *us* is God the Father, God the Son, and God the Holy Spirit. Yes, they are three in one. We can all agree that we came from somewhere and that somewhere is God. He told you in Luke 1:31 that the Virgin Mary shall conceive in her womb and bring forth a son, and we shall call his name *Jesus*. If you can't believe it with your own mind, then you must believe it by faith, otherwise you can't walk in wisdom.

Since you refuse to walk in wisdom, there is no other alternative except deception. To all the unbelievers today, what I believe has happened based upon my relationship with our Lord and Savior Jesus Christ, is because of unbelief. God has allowed us to be deceived in every way that does not give Him Glory.

The rulers of darkness rule this world today. Who are they, everyone who exalts themselves over Christ? If the masons, fraternities, and sororities are of secret societies, and I am not either of the three, then how can I know their secret, except if the Holy Spirit tells me or show me? Granted the life that God has given me to live has been everything but good, and yet I believe. It would be easy for me to not to believe in Jesus Christ. If I had believed the lies of the enemy, I would be a total mess. I am totally convinced that Jesus Christ is Lord.

Because of my belief in Christ, I was able to help set the captive free, which was my daughter when the enemies were trying to attack her mind. I was successful because of my obedience to Christ. As I close this chapter, I would hope that I have been a help to you as I continue to walk in God's love until the rapture comes for me. In the name of Jesus I pray. Amen! Receive your blessings that the Lord has waiting for you as you seek wisdom. It is yours for the asking. The Bible says the truth shall make you free, and he that is free is free indeed.

THE SPIRIT OF REJECTION

I remember when I was a little girl before the age of kindergarten, I was home alone with my grandmother on my mother's side. My mother was gone to work. I do not recall my father being present at this time, but I know that there was no grandfather ever present in my life. I do not recall my grandmother ever being kind to me. The spirit of Christ taught me that my grandmother opened the door for the spirit of rejection to take root in my life, and that is how rejection was birth into my life. This spirit often times caused me to feel unwanted because my grandmother was never nice to me. As a result of rejection, I grew up with negative feelings (spirits) that were attached to me, such as always feeling excluded from whatever was going on. With rejection, betrayal and shame goes hand in hand. The enemy knew what God had in store for me, and it was his plan to execute the plan of God, but his plan did not work.

The spirit of rejection causes us not to be able to love the way God intended for us to love because of negative emotions. The reason people are not able to love one another is because of resentment, hatred, and rebellion. In 1 Samuel 15:23, it tells us that rebellion is the spirit of witchcraft. For a long time, I resented the family I was born into until our Lord and savior Jesus Christ allowed me to see that life is about where I choose to spend my eternal life. This means that God does what he wants to do when he wants to and how he wants to do it. I don't believe I harbored hatred in my heart toward others. It was hatred about how people treated me, but it was still hatred, which is a negative spirit. The way I rebelled was I did not do what others did if I did not think it was right in the sight of God, which caused me to look like I had a stand off spirit. I was oftentimes seen by myself. That was because not many people wanted to hear the truth.

Once the Lord set me free from the spirit of rejection, my whole life began to unfold before my eyes. It was as if my eyes were opened to the truth, which is of God. As apart of my healing process, I discovered that I am a writer by nature. I knew in my heart that God would one day use me to get a message to his people. The message would be "search your own heart" and be set free. God wants us to trust him and know that for every problem, there is an answer. Here is a good reason in the face of rejection to send it back to the pits of hell where it originated from:

> For I am persuaded, that neither death, nor life, nor angels, nor principalities, nor powers, nor things present, nor things to come, nor height, nor depth, nor any other creature, shall be able to separate us from the love of God, which is in Christ Jesus our Lord. (Rom. 8:38–39)

Once we come to the knowledge of the truth, the spirit of rejection will have no power in your life. Psalm 34:8 says, "O taste and see that the Lord is good: blessed is the man that trusts in Him."

My friend, another truth about rejection is that the people that lived during the time that Jesus walked the earth in the flesh, and every person born until this day, who have not yet accepted Christ today, has rejected Jesus so you now have something in common with Jesus. If you have not accepted Christ as Lord and Savior of your life, read *Romans 10:9;* this is how we are saved. Then read *John 3:16;* this is why we are saved. Once your rejection is dealt with, and you learn how to curse your rejection from the root, that would be a done deal in the spirit of Christ. The Bible says all things work together for the good to them that love God and are called according to his purpose. Just trust him.

YOU WERE NOT ABANDONED

I discovered in my healing process that abandonment is one of the biggest lies satan ever convinced us with. Our Heavenly Father who is in Heaven loves each of us so much until he made sure since the beginning of time that we understand that we have not been abandoned. Case and point, to be abandoned means that someone gave up on you, which left you feeling unloved and rejected. This cannot be true because in Hebrews 13:5, "God promised never to leave us or forsake us." Not only that, Jeremiah 29:11 says, "For I know the plans I have for you declares the Lord, plans to prosper you and not to harm you and plans to give you hope and a future." When you thought or felt that you were abandoned, you really were not because your Heavenly Father was there all the time.

On Easter Sunday morning in 1972, when my mother got me dressed for Church, she sent me along with my other siblings around the corner from where we lived to Mount Calvary Baptist Church on Spruce Street. By the time Church was over, and we got home, the ambulance had already taken her to the hospital. That was very sudden and was the last time I'd seen her alive. The next time I saw her, she was lying in a casket. Not many days after her funeral, my father walked away with out saying goodbye. At that time that was a double abandonment, and the enemy used that as a part of my bondage until I came into the knowledge of truth. As a result of the abandonments, I was left to continue to live with my grandmother. I thank God for Psalms 27:10–14.

I truly believe that everything we face in life is apart of our journey. The Lord uses it for Him to get the glory out of it if we encounter it with his Holy Spirit. Our ancestors use to call it the Holy Ghost. The Holy Spirit's function is to lead and guide us into all truth. The Lord was pressing on my heart to confront the enemy during this time in my life, so I did. My grandmother was growing old, and sickness came upon her I believe from old age. She was then hospitalized.

Before she was hospitalized, me, my siblings, and other family members took turns keeping her in our homes or apartments to keep her from being placed into the nursing home. Not long before that time, I was taking my grandmother to a doctor's appointment and I asked my grandmother all the questions I wanted to know because I knew at some point God was going to call her home. My thinking was at that time was if I did not ask her what I needed to know while she was living, so that when God called her home, the enemy could not tamper with my mind because the answer came from her. That way there could not be any doubt about why she treated me so mean.

I said to my grandmother in love, "Grandma, why were you so mean to me when I was a child?"

She responded, "I was mad at Ruth (my mother) for dying and leaving me to take care of nine children by myself."

I said, "oh!"

At that point, I was okay because I probably would have felt the same way. I was not looking for a right or wrong answer. I was only looking for her truth because it mattered.

> Isaiah 1:18–20: Says come now, and let us reason together, saith the Lord: though your sins be as scarlet, they shall be as white as snow; though they be red like crimson, they shall be as wool. If ye be willing and obedient, ye shall eat the good of the land: but if ye refuse and rebel, ye shall be devoured with the sword: for the mouth of the Lord hath spoken it.

The way this Bible explains these three verses are: The Lord presented two options to the people. One was to repent and obey. A remarkable transformation would result. Now they were blood red as a result of their sin, but repentance would turn them a glorious *white*. They could be cleansed with the result that life would be good. The second option was continued rebellion, a course of action that would end with their destruction.

During the same time when I asked my grandmother in love about her relationship to me, I had the opportunity to ask my earthly father in love what I needed to know at that time. I asked my father, "Why did you walk away and leave me when my mother died?"

My earthly father answered me and said, "I left because of your sister, Winkey (Paula)."

When he said that, he did not have to say anymore because I knew what kind of sister she was to me. Then my earthly father went on to tell me about his childhood. He said to me when he was a baby, he was left on the doorstep of the father he knew.

He went on to say that father raised him until around the age of sixteen or seventeen until his known father died. After that, my earthly father said he had to pretty much steal food to eat until he signed himself up to go into the service, which part I am not sure. I know that part is true because I have his United States of America flag in my closet. He also told me that when he got out of the service, his wrongdoing caught up with him, so he had to do time for whatever he did. With all of that being said, I learned some valuable information by not holding animosity in my heart about nothing. Although the abandonment was a reality in my life from my earthly father, my maternal grandmother and mother was real, but the love of Jesus Christ was greater. Because of the love of Christ, I loved them until death.

What I have discovered concerning abandonment is that nothing happens unless God allowed it to happen. Once we understand that nothing in this life is about us, and understand everything is either about Jesus Christ or satan, then and only then your double mind must exit your head. Since life is a journey, do you agree that it is easier to focus on one person or two people? I believe it would be easier to focus on one person. No matter what no man tells you concerning your destiny, once you choose what has been written in the Holy Bible who you will serve, your life would make more sense to you. The Holy Bible teaches us in *Isaiah 1:18* to "come now let us reason together." For the people or persons in your life that caused a spirit of abandonment in your life, there are many lessons that can be learned from it. Let God have His way in your life today.

My earthly father, for example, because of the life God allowed him to be born into was never dealt with in the manner God intended. I say this because what he shared with me concerning his life at the latter part of his life was very deep. Had he dealt with it properly, he would have made sure to have had a relationship with his children. Instead, he had a relationship with alcohol and the people that hung at CK's Liquor on the corner of Myrtle Avenue and Beaver Street.

CK's Liquor is where I went one Wednesday night after Bible Study and made him come go with me. He was so drunk that I took him to the emergency room for detox. At that time, he had a pint of liquor in his pocket, but that did not matter, what mattered was he needed help. From there, he went to the nursing home at Eartha White until he died seven years later. He accepted Christ before he died. He thanked me for what I did for him in spite of what kind of father he was to me.

We really don't have a right to hold animosity in our hearts because of what whoever has done to us. God told us to "choose life." Holding animosity causes heart disease, which will kill you. You cannot afford to give no one that kind of power in your life. When you think about it, everyday Jesus is speaking to us, telling us to do something. We walk away from Him like he never said a word to us. He loves us so much, and He is calling us every day to come to Him because life is so much better with Him. Those he is speaking to don't listen, and that is abandonment to our Lord and savior Jesus Christ. Read Romans 10:9 and John 3:16. I love you. God bless you!

Thank You, God, for My Pain

The Bible says in John 16:33, "In this world you will have tribulation (pain); but be of good cheer, I (Christ) have overcome the world." Everyone will experience pain at sometime in their lives whether it be emotional, physical, or spiritual. The reason being is that God wants to get the glory out of every situation whether it is positive or negative. If our journey is predestined, then it means that there is purpose in our pain. No one in their right mind wishes pain on themselves. As I think about the reality my life, how it has been from the beginning until this day, I give God all of the glory that is due to Him. Anyone who really knows me knows that I have seen many trials in my days. I am writing this book today because God has been so faithful to me. The pain in my life has taught me to give God praise in all things.

Pain is a tool I have discovered in my life that God uses in our lives to see what degree we will love and trust Him for Him to get His glory. God created everything and everyone, which means everything belongs to Him. So, since everything belongs to my Heavenly Father, there is nothing except one thing any of us can give Him. We can't give Him a round trip ticket to any place because he is already everywhere. We can't give him no money, it is already his. No car, nothing tangible, everything is already his. The only thing my Heavenly Father can't give himself is *praise*. That is the ultimate reason we were created is to praise God. This is why I can thank God for my pain.

Although, I experienced much pain in my life, the Lord bought back to my attention the most painful situation ever in my life. The situation took place twenty-eight years prior to the time this book was written. The pain was the murder of my youngest daughter (Tamoka Spencer) 1979–1991. Praise God! The day before this part of this book was written, satan used my best friend since the second grade, she was there when my daughter was murdered.

The attack was not about my friend and I, the attack was from satan to break me down. I knew Jesus too well to have let that happen. So I took it in, love. My Heavenly Father, who loves me so much, fixed the situation immediately. He said, "Yes, true, your best friend went there. Remember, all of the glory belongs to me. Your daughter was twelve years old when I allowed satan to have his way in Tamoka's life. I allowed that. "Daughter, remember when you were seventeen years old and you were pregnant with Tamoka and you already had two other children, Marlon and Twana at seventeen years old? You did not want the *shame*, but you did it for me because you loved me so much." I said, "Yes, Lord."

God said to me, "Remember, daughter, when you told your children's daddy you were pregnant with Tamoka"? Their daddy told his mom, his mom in return told the preacher, I guess to hide the truth and to protect me from further embarrassment. They arranged for me to have an abortion. I could not get it done in Jacksonville because I was too far along. They found a place in Miami, took me there to have an abortion. But *praise God,* when the doctor came in to talk to me, remembering I was 17 years old, the love of God that lived inside of me at seventeen years old said to the doctor, "No, sir, I do not want no abortion."

With this being said, when the enemy tried to rise up against me, my Heavenly Father taught me how to ease the pain. The way I look at my daughter demise, satan's intent was to kill her at birth, but God said no! Satan never gave up. Around twelve years later, God let satan have his way and let satan kill her. God knew he would still get the glory, honor, and praise from me.

The only way a child could end up pregnant at age fourteen is because she had to have been visited by a sexual demon before or during the conception. The sexual demon most of the time is birthed from an adult that goes undealt with. I've come to set the captives free, *praise God!* Once we release the bondage of pain, we can all be set free. Once we decide to be in right relationship first with God and then others, we enter into the life of total peace. The kind of peace that surpasses all understanding that can only come through the love of Jesus Christ. Another truth I've learned about hurt and pain is that hurt and pain is a true but negative spirit.

The word of God teaches us that God is a Spirit. They that worship Him must worship Him in Spirit and in truth. The discovery is that when hurt and or pain visit us, the moment we recognize it, all we have to do is release it to our Heavenly Father as quickly as possible. We must cut hurt and pain down to the root. God is so amazing. The moment I do this, I say something like, "God you know I love you, or Jesus you know I love you, have your own way Father in my life." Saying these words or anything like this is worshiping or praising the Trinity, meaning the Father, Son, and Holy Spirit. Learn how to not let satan have his way with you in your life. Love you, and God bless you!

Praise God from who *all* blessings flow. When you think of pain, don't think of it just when someone hurts you or even when you hurt someone. Let's think of pain in sickness for one moment. People of God, we have been bamboozled for a long time. It is time to live our lives the way our Heavenly Father intended us to live.

In Proverbs 17:22, it reads, "A merry heart does good *like* a medicine; but, a broken spirit dries the bones." What laughter does is it triggers the release of endorphins, the body's natural feel-good chemicals that our Heavenly Father placed inside of us when He created us. Endorphins promote an overall sense of well-being and can even temporarily relieve pain. Laughter also protects the heart. Endorphins are our body's natural painkillers and can boost our moods.

Glory to God in the highest! At the age of fifty-six years old, I can work your nerves if you don't know me in the Spirit of Jesus Christ. I don't believe in medications, but maybe in the case of an emergency. In my mind, if Jesus Christ is the healer and he was crucified on that cross for us, to me, it is a lie what they want me to believe about medicine. Question, whose report will you believe? I thank God for his anointing because his anointing destroys the *yoke* of bondage. I am one of those old saints of God with the ridiculous faith. Not only that, *God is so awesome!* He knows the *end* from the *beginning*. He *rules*, and he *super rules*.

When he allowed me to know my purpose in life, the sky was the limit in what I can have. My purpose in life is to give *God the glory in all things*, the good and the bad things I encounter in life. So when he created me, he knew that he was creating a worshiper in Him. That is why He allowed so much to happen to me in my life. He knew if He allowed it, He knew I was still going to praise Him. God had to send me through so many awful, painful situations in life so that when he gets ready to bless me, I will not turn on him.

In Genesis 8:22, the Bible teaches us that as long as the earth remains, there will be *seed time* and *harvest*, cold and heat, summer and winter, day and night. Since God is not a man, that he shall lie, neither is he the Son of man, that he shall repent. If he said something, it has to come to pass. In *Galatians 6:7,* it says you reap what you sow. I found it to be a blessing to have faced so many horrible trails. In each horrible trail, I *gave* God his glory. The word of God tells me as long as we are on this earth, there will be seed and harvest time. This book is an indicator of my harvest. I've sown many good seeds in my life. I see the rest of my life living in over flow. If I sowed (seed) pain for most of my life and if a (harvest) must come from what I sow, which means my harvest is here based on this book. God knows it was painful, but I received it in love, in the name of *Jesus*.

THE PAST FAILURES ARE THE FUTURE BLESSINGS

The rape and the molestations, the Lord allowed in the beginning of my life, left me traumatized. The trauma I experienced as a child, that lying spirit would always try to rise against me in school when it was time to learn. Remember in the chapter where I talked about being a mother at the age of fourteen years old. Because I had a son, I was told school was no place for me. So it took me a long time to get a high school education. The reason it took me so long is because of the attacks of the mind, from the lying spirit.

I refused to believe that I was not smart and could not learn. I told myself no matter how long it takes, I will get a high school education, and I did. The moment I received my diploma, I went to the community college and received an Associate in Science Degree in Elementary Education. I went on to receive a Bachelor of business Administration Organizational Management Degree. After then, I still was not sure of my purpose in life at that time. I thought I was to become a nurse, which I tried before and failed at it. So I went back to school, and I became a licensed practical nurse.

In one of the previous chapters, I told you after working at Shands Jacksonville for twenty plus years, my elder brother, Jesus, made up a reason for me to get fired. The reason he made up was not in my character. I knew from that moment he had a work for me to do. This is why it is so important to be lead by the Spirit of Christ (the Holy Ghost). The negative spirit I felt did not want me to know that God created me with intelligence in the word of God. That was what the battle I felt in my mind was about. Once I came into the knowledge of the truth about life itself, it taught me that my Heavenly Father do not create unintelligent people.

My Heavenly Father creates his children with a measure of faith. The Bible says faith without works is dead. Faith is how I lived my life in the face of adversity. I knew once I allowed the Holy Spirit to have his way in my life by not taking offense to what happened to me in my life, but knowing it was the will of my Heavenly Father, then it was time for me to reap a harvest. When you are lead by the Spirit, the areas you think you failed in will posses blessings that are not seen in the flesh, but are seen in the Spirit of Christ.

In the areas I failed in my life, at my Heavenly Father's appointed time, he let me see how smart I am. The Holy Spirit's function is to lead us and guide us into all truth. I did that, and the Holy Spirit began to show me things I should not have known, except He showed it to me, which allows me to appear smart to others, but it's really the Holy Spirit. Each of us can do all things in Christ who gives us the strength to do so. In all your ways, acknowledge Him, and He shall direct your path. Trust in the Lord and lean not on your own understanding, and he shall direct your path. Oh! Taste and see that the Lord is good. Bless the Lord oh my soul and all that is within me, bless His holy name. He's worthy of all the glory, all the honor, and all the praise.

I believe as it relates to my education, my Heavenly Father was protecting me from what goes on at the top. He wants to show His people how life is supposed to be lived as he intended. There is no way I could know what goes on at the top if I have never been to the top. The only way I could know what goes on at the top is the Lord showing it to me. This is what my Heavenly Father in the name of his darling Son Jesus Christ showed me. At the top, secret societies were created from the pagan gods. I could not be a part of that, yet he showed me the truth about it.

My Heavenly Father loves us so much. He does not want anyone to perish (die) with out being born again. We must understand the truth before it is too late. When Christ walked this earth for thirty- three years and ascended up to sit at the right hand of the Father, He told His disciples before He left that "He would be back."

The pagan gods don't want the secret society members to know He is truly coming back. They did not like Jesus then, and they don't like him now. My Lord is coming back for His people.

THE GIFT OF
DISCERNMENT IS
NOT CRITICISM

Everyone who makes it a habit to walk close with Jesus Christ will have a gift of discernment. This gift will show you who's who in the Spirit. You will oftentimes find yourself being accused of knowing it all. Do not let that hurt your feelings. It is the Christ that lives inside of you that knows it all. Criticism is critiquing someone in a negative sense without biblical explanation. Discernment is seeing or knowing something as the Lord showed it to you. For it is written in the word of God that we must not be ignorant of nothing. Whatever comes to your mind will be sent either from Christ or satan. The more you spend time with Christ, the more you will know his voice. He says, "My sheep hears my voice and a stranger they will not follow." The voice of Jesus Christ is not going to tell you anything wrong. The voice of satan is not going to tell you anything right.

We must learn to build each other up in love and see one another the way God sees us. God does not see us the way that we are, He sees us the way that we will be when he does the work in us. There are some people that no matter what you say, they will take it in a negative way. This will happen when demonic forces have taken up residence inside their heads, and they choose to believe a lie. This type of person will need you to keep praying for them until they get a break through from the Lord. The gift of discernment can be a tool that will keep us in the *ark of safety* for the rest of our lives. That still small voice you hear that tells you don't go that way, go the other way, and you find out later someone got killed, that is discernment. Because you were obedient to the Spirit of Christ, your life was spared and someone else lost their life.

Not that it is good for anyone to be killed, but listening to the words of Christ is what is important. Constructive criticism is the process of offering valid and well-reasoned opinions about the work of others, usually involving both positive and negative comments, in a friendly manner rather than an oppositional one. Spiritual discernment produces healing in areas of our lives that has been or could be wounded. Remember whatever we do or say in life. do it or say it in love. It will make a world of difference. Let it be your attempt to always build up and never tear down.

We must ask for forgiveness for our known sins as well as the unknown sins we commit every day. We can offend others and not realize we have offended them. The Lord's Prayer says, "After God gives us our daily bread, forgive us our trespasses as we forgive those that trespass against us." The Lord's Prayer in its entirety is found in Matthew 6:9–13. I believe each of us should be quick to forgive others when they do wrong to us. If we do not forgive others, we will not be forgiven when we do wrong to others. *Unforgiveness* can be linked to heart disease and undiagnosed heart trouble. Let whatever you have been holding on to go today and choose life. By refusing to let go, if God sends his Son to get his children today, you will not go with him because of the sin of unforgiveness. Let it go, and continue to receive your blessings.

THE SAINTS WILL KNOW IF THE HOLY GHOST IS INSIDE

The main function of the Holy Ghost is to lead you and guide you into all truth. The Holy Ghost is referred to as (He). The part of my journey, after I learned my purpose in life, he allowed me to see life for what it really is. My purpose in life is to worship Jesus Christ in such a way that will allow me to be used to set the captives free. I have so much confidence in Jesus Christ that I will not fear nothing or no one even if it cost me my life. For Christ, I will live and for Christ I will die. Blessed be the name of the Lord.

I never had a desire to reach the top although I knew that I was different. Nothing can happen to me unless God allows it to happen, so I am just going to tell you how the Holy Ghost told it to me. A lot of the people that make it to the top are apart of what they call The Secret Society, masons, fraternities, and sororities. My question to any of the members is, "If it is a secret society, how do I know so much about it if I am not a member?" The secret would be expected to stay within the members only, right?

The Holy Ghost directed me through the path that lead me to people with the information I need to build a strong case for my Heavenly Father. I did my research as well. It is not my intent to cause anyone to be upset, but it is my intent to expose the enemy at all cost. Yes, even if it cost me my life, I doubt it very seriously. Heaven is real, and so is hell. I have been given the biblical duty to make sure as many people as I possibly can know this truth.

Here are the facts taken from the book, *The Hiram Key*, written by Chris Knight and Robert Lomas. Point 1: the people who join the masons do not understand a word of the ceremonies they participate in, and their only fear is that people would laugh at the pointless and silly rituals they perform. Point 2: there are many degrees; at the end, you denounce who or what you have always believed in and accept their pagan god. There are many other points. This is the last one I will share with you. Point 3: the promise that is made to the members of the secret societies are they will look out for each other in this society whether a situation is right or wrong.

The word of God tells us that we are not to have other gods before Him. He says, "He is a Jealous God, and He will not share His glory with no other god." Today, if you hear the Lord talking to you, please do not harden your heart. At God's appointed time, He would look to his right and say, "Son! Go get my children." The Bible says that even His Son does not know when this time will be. All I know is that every prophecy, except this one, has already been fulfilled. Christ coming could be any moment. Christ does not want any of us to be left behind. I am not writing this on my own. The Holy Ghost that lives inside of me is directing me to do so. If you don't know what to do or say, just repeat these words, "Father, in the name of Jesus, I come to you as humble as I know how, asking you to please forgive me of every sin I omitted and committed against you. Father, I denounce the fraternity, sorority or freemason I joined, not understanding what I was getting myself into. I accept Jesus Christ as Lord and savior of my life. In the name of Jesus I pray, amen!"

Because of the confession you have just made, you are now saved. Ask the Heavenly Father to direct you to a Church that teaches and preach Jesus Christ and Him crucified on the cross. Read 1 Thessalonians 4:16–18:

> For the Lord Himself shall descend from Heaven
> with a shout, with the voice of the archangel, and
> with the trump of God: and the dead in Christ
> shall rise first: then we which are alive and remain
> shall be caught up together with them in the

clouds, to meet the Lord in the air: and so shall we ever be with the Lord. Therefore comfort one another with these words.

Now I See

It's been seven months ago since I sat down to complete this information that has been given to me concerning these things that are true because I love God with all my heart, mind, and soul. He walks with me, and he talks with me. He tells me that I am His own. When the Lord opened my eyes to the reality of life as it should be as opposed to the way it really is, I was amazed. Only God can let us see every situation as it should be seen. It is true many of us see the truth, but often times it is too late. It is not that God is not talking to us, we are not listening to Him. Why, because of our daily habits and the way we live life.

The way our Heavenly Father presented the truth about the church to me and everything since the beginning of time gave me the courage to stand no matter what. It caused me to understand about my beginnings and anyone else's who do not understand what is going on. I have been accused of thinking I know everything by people God allows me to meet. It is not that I know everything, it is because of my relationship with Christ. My prayer is that who ever read what I am writing will understand that if God is all knowing, it is up to him to share his words with whom he chooses. He knows who loves Him and who doesn't, who will talk to Him and who will not. So, if I stay in His presence as much as possible, why wouldn't He share with me? The word of God says that He will not withhold no good thing from His people.

Today, I am free. There are no more chains holding me. I am no more bound by anything. I thank God for setting me free. I have been free for a long time now. I knew God was ready to elevate me the day I leaned over the casket and kissed my sister goodbye. She was the one that satan used to try to destroy me when I was a child.

She was forgiven long before then. I made sure I let her know that long before she passed away. Not only her but my father and grandmother as well. At my sister's funeral, when I leaned over to kiss her goodbye, I knew it was not her who wronged me when I was a child, it was satan himself. Satan's goal was to destroy me because he knew that our Heavenly Father was going to use me to help set the captives free. The hurt, shame, and pain I felt because of what happened to me is no longer a reality in my life. Only God can allow that to happen, and he wants to do that for every person that the enemy came against if we let him do it. Let go and let God have his way. It cannot and will not be done without Jesus the Christ.

FORGIVE US OUR KING

Before the fall of Adam and Eve, our father created us into this world that represented genuine love. We were given everything we needed to exist. After the fall mankind wanted to be equal to God. After the flood with Noah and the Ark from that moment, the tower of Babel was built as rebellion against God about the flood.

The descendants of Noah said that they were going to build a tower that would reach Heaven so that they could make a name for themselves. So, the Lord came down to see what they were doing and said, "if they would build a tower to reach Heaven, then nothing they do will be impossible." So the Lord confused their language so they wouldn't understand each other and scattered them over the face of the whole earth. You can find all of this written in the Bible. Now, here is what the Lord told and showed me concerning what I have written in this book. Remember a few chapters back in this book? I love the word of God and try to do what he tells me to do to the best of my ability. When my Heavenly Father opened my eyes about His church, I was so amazed and loved Him even more.

The masons, fraternities, sororities, and eastern stars have built a name for themselves. They have been tricked into this lifestyle believing that they rule the world. Once they are initiated in, they are not told what they are really getting themselves into until the very end of being an official member. These members must bow down to their leader and denounce their God as they know him. They must give their hearts, mind, and soul to the god of their mason, fraternity, or sorority.

As it was told to me by the Holy Ghost, their god is Hiram Abiff and Athena Minerva. This is the reason why they refer to themselves as a secret society. With all of this being said, they are worshiping pagan gods, which means they are worshiping demons. This is the reason why the world is in the condition that it is in today. Every since Jesus Christ ascended up to sit in the seat at the right hand of the Father, mankind wanted to take His place on Earth. The word of God tells us that He would not with hold no good thing from His people. The fact that anything has to be a secret tells us it is wrong in the sight of God. In almost everything that connects us together in this world at the top, it is someone that is connected to one of the secret societies. Unless it was built on faith in God, the big "G" God.

Please allow me to prophesy for a moment. In the church, I will use my church where I have sat for the last twenty-nine years. My now Bishop and First Lady, who I love dearly and would do anything in reason for, are a part of a fraternity and a sorority. Although they are, they still stand in the name of Jesus Christ. The Bible tells us we cannot serve two masters, we either love one and hate the other, or we hate one and love the other. So this tells us that something is seriously wrong in the church. We can all see that something is seriously wrong in our countries, states, cities, and towns. Not to mention the schools and families. If the people that sit in the seats of high places really are concerned about what is going on, they would first, listen, and second, turn from what is wrong to what is right. If not, one day soon, our Heavenly Father will look to His right in the seat of His Son, "our elder brother" and say, "Son go get my children." Then we shall behold him face-to-face, our Savior and Lord. Those that remain will be left here to be tormented by satan worst than what it is now. It is called the tribulation.

In the church, most people worship the leader and do not know Christ. This is the way it was designed to be not in the early days but since things began to change in the church the way our ancestors knew it. Back to the beginning of this book, from my childhood, no one would be able to see the love of the Lord in that. God knows what he is doing. Each of our lives is a journey, and our journey will never be completed without the beginning, middle, and end of our lives. This would be a perfect time for each of us to make our wrongs right with our Lord and Savior, Jesus the Christ. He longs to have a personal relationship with each of us. He loves us.

This can be done by simply opening up the door of our hearts and let Him come in today. In Revelation 3:20, it shows Jesus talking to every person in this world. He says, "I stand at the door of your heart knocking, if any man open up his or her heart and let Me in, I will come in and live with you." Here is the proof for anyone that has not been born again as of today, this means that satan is your lord, and you do exactly what he tells you to do. This is what the world being in turmoil is all about, the killing, raping, abuse, lying, stealing, and etc., is all about. My conviction is the family I was born into, which is the family God wanted me to be born into, coupled with what this world had to offer me. My creation made a whole lot of sense in relation to existence, rejection, and acceptance.

THE HEALING
FOR MY SOUL

My interpretation of my existence is this, God created me with Ruth Silas and Willie Johnson. Notice they are not married. Although I do not know much about the two. My mother died suddenly after getting me dressed for church Easter Sunday morning in 1972. My father walked away after the funeral, never to have been seen again until about eighteen years later when I saw him walking down the sidewalk with a walker going to the liquor store on the corner of Myrtle Ave and Beaver Street in Jacksonville, Florida. Surely I picked him up to give him a ride to his destination.

Had I not picked him up, I would not have gotten all the information I needed to write this book some twenty-five or twenty-six years later, give or take a few. That was God orchestrating a part of my journey. After my mother died and I was left to live with my grandmother, who wasn't happy about the situation and where I found myself, I was pregnant at the age of thirteen and gave birth at the age of fourteen. The same thing, had I not asked my grandmother the questions I did way back in my young adult days, I could not write this book. This was God again orchestrating a part of my life.

Many people think that they have to be a part of something before they can feel like they belong. That is so not true. Let us use education for an example, do not get me wrong, knowledge is power. Society wants you to believe that you must go to college, and the Bible does say to render unto Ceasar that which belongs to Ceasar. Also, render unto God that which belongs to God. For me, when I stepped out on faith and received my Bachelor's Degree in Organizational Management, all praises are due to God.

I say that because the Dean of girls at Robert E. Lee told me that school was no place for me. I did not believe that the same demonic forces that planted the seeds in the territory in 1976 haunted me a long time. Yet my God was faithful to me, and He saw me through. On the other hand, the Bachelor's Degree is just on the shelf, and I am paying back a huge debt because of it. I believe God is going to see me through the debt as well. This is what happens in society as it relates to education. They teach you of the many pagan gods, and then they encourage you to join the fraternities and sororities. After you are recruited and become a member, then you initiate someone else to worship pagan gods, which are demon spirits.

This is the same thing that is happening in the church today, this same concept. Church members are being deceived, worshiping man and not Jesus Christ. After all the heartaches, rejection, and pain I have encountered in my life, I find that all of it was necessary for the coming of Jesus Christ. I had to endure so much pain in the beginning and the middle of my journey until the beginning of the end of my journey is fun. There is no more pain nowhere; it is just sorrow now. The sorrow is about the deception of people and what took place with the pagan gods. God has proven himself to be faithful to me in every way I needed him to be. I feel like a ninja in the Spirit of Christ.

I have gone through so much in my lifetime with no one but Jesus Christ to be with me. Nothing can make me doubt our Father who art in heaven. I have that kind of peace that surpasses all understanding that the Bible speaks of. I plan to spend the rest of my life on assignment for Christ alone. I believe God choose me for this journey because he knew I would continue to love him no matter what, so he tried my faith. Another part of my healing was when God showed me the important information of the generational curses in my family. Because what was shown to me allowed me to be set free from the hidden sins.

We must keep in mind that God has a plan and a purpose for our lives. It is hard for some people to believe that God loves us so much until he himself came down from heaven and walked this earth as Jesus the Christ. He had to come as his son because if he had come as himself, we would have died just to have laid eyes on him.

In the book of Exodus 33:12–23, it says:

> God said that Moses had found favor with Him. Moses said to the Lord "If you are pleased with me, teach me your ways so I may continue to find favor with you Lord." Moses said to the Lord, (remember that this nation is your people. "The Lord replied back to Moses, "My presence will go with you Moses." Then Moses said back to the Lord, "If your Presence does not go with us, do not send us up from here." Moses said to God again, "How will anyone know that you are pleased with me and your people unless you go with us?" Moses is still speaking, "What else will distinguish me and your people from all the other people on the face of the Earth?" So, the Lord said to Moses, "I will do the very thing you have asked, because I am pleased with you and I know you by name." Then Moses said to God, "Now show me your glory." Moses wanted to see what God look like.
>
> Then God said to Moses, "Alright, I will cause all my goodness (backside) to pass in front of you, and I will proclaim my name, the Lord, in your presence. I will have mercy on whom I will have mercy, and compassion on whom I will have compassion." Then God said to Moses, "But, you cannot see my face, for no one may see me and live." So, the Lord told Moses, "There is a place near Me where you may stand on a rock. When My glory passes by, I will put you in a cleft in the rock and cover you with my hand until I have passed by. Then I will remove my hand and you will see my back; but My face must not be seen."

I wrote this to give you a better understanding as to who God truly is. Again, God loves us so much until he came from heaven to earth just to show us the way and yet we don't believe. The same way after Jesus ascended up to be with the Father and sent the Holy Spirit to live inside of those who believe in him. That is the same function of what we see today as it relates to the evil we see happening now, the evil spirit flowing from satan and his representatives who carries the same function. Jesus said that he is coming back to receive us unto himself one day. I believe the time is closer now than it has ever been.

ABOUT THE AUTHOR

I am amazed of just how much God loves each of His people. Reflecting back over my life, there was a time I had no direction as to who I was. I did not know which way to go. Realizing now, God was leading and guiding me all the time. Today, I have no doubt of where I am or which way I must go. Because of my life experiences, I know the voice of God. Where He leads I will follow. I have learned to consult with Him before I make important decisions for the rest of my life. I have learned that God will show Himself in the Spirit realm to everyone that desires to have a true relationship with Him. Because of the love of God, I have no fear, and I will fear no man upon this earth. I will respect every man, women, boy, and girl that lives. The only one I will fear is God Himself since he can destroy the body and the soul. I will not fear. Although we are living in the last days according to the Bible, for God I will live, and for God I will die. Blessed be the name of the Lord! Amen.